Ta

Breath
And FOCUS

By Brandon McIntosh

CONTENTS

Take A Deep Breath
And FOCUS

Objective: to learn focus, to build an attitude of excellence and to lay a foundation of successful habits.

Definition: I recognize my potential and that there is expectation over my life; I am committed to being my best.
I am willing to learn more. I desire to excel. I do not need anything to define who I am.

I AM RELENTLESS.

Introduction

Why I Wrote This Book

It's not that I want to write this book. It's more like I have to write this book. I would wake up thinking about it. It's me leaving something behind for my son Kingston.

These are the things that were shared with me as I processed and weighed my past behaviors next to my present mentality, because I wanted to produce a different future outcome.

This is me challenging myself, challenging you, questioning, critiquing and facing myself. Out of all that, I have produced a manual by which you can reach goals, and change behavior to match what your purpose is.

 I have been wanting to write this book for some time now. I spent a lot of my young life planning, strategizing and fantasizing. The process to even get to the place where I was ready to write things down was a struggle.

The inspiration behind this book was almost in a different reality that no one around me seemed to believe existed. I believe it exists. I believe it exists and I fantasized, I prayed. I couldn't sleep, couldn't rest because this relentless approach, relentless mindset seemed to meet me when I was tired and I had to get up in the morning.

 This is why I procrastinated, because I saw so much. The information was so immense and it was hard to process it at first. I am ready to share now, but more than that I want to plant something in you that will help you pursue your purpose. Beyond your limitations, beyond what you can see, I want to push you, motivate you past your pain, your hurt and fears.

When I was younger, I was the tallest kid in my circle. Everyone else was small, and they wore smaller clothes. It was easier for them to buy clothes, because their shoes were small.

I didn't feel I fit in because I was taller than everyone else. So, I would wear too small shoes to try to fit in. The issue was that my feet were bigger and I needed a bigger size.

The problem was I was bigger, and my shoulders were broader than theirs. Anytime you allow who you are to be defined by people who are smaller than you, you will be in pain and be limited for the rest of your life. It's time to reach out and…

Be Relentless.

I had a recurring dream that is the inspiration behind this book. I can't say that I had that dream every night, but I would have the same dream often.

Having the dream often and in the same way was what really caused me to move past my feelings about what I was dreaming about and work to hear and understand what I was being presented.

I must be honest -- this dream was intimidating! I didn't want to talk about it or have the dream anymore.

Chapter 1
The Dream

The dream has different phases to it. At the beginning, I was back on the basketball court in a game. The game is always competitive, but before the game is complete, I wake up. I am not able to run as fast and jump as high in this particular game, but I am present.

The next part of the dream puts me back in high school on the football field. I stopped playing football my sophomore year of high school. That decision to stop playing football was a decision made from fatigue.

So, the dream puts me back in high school playing football. At the time I was having the dream, I found it exciting. But as the dream ended, I would wake up disappointed.

I was disappointed because I had made the wrong decision. If I had made the wrong decision, why did I choose wrong and what were the leading factors that caused that decision?

Then the process of understanding the dream started. I kept it to myself, searching within and processing what seemed like every day. It seemed as though my whole life was summed up in that recurring dream.

Something in that dream was enticing and intriguing. It was a very crucial time for me to work and uncover something hidden inside of something that I didn't even know was there.

One day, as I was walking to the gym to play basketball, for the first time, I suddenly realized and understood so clearly the purpose and/or reason for the recurring dream.

I realized that there was something to pass on here, something that would help and coach other people to complete and be better prepared to make adjustments and enjoy the ride in the process.

The walk to the gym was passionate and intense. I imagine that the drivers driving on my side of the road thought I was crazy. I was moving my mouth as if I were talking to someone, and moving my hands and arms as if I was directing traffic.

I dreamed about sports, but the lesson was about life and the Xs and Os of it all. It was a mental and psychological adjustment that I was going through.

This reoccurring dream challenged my thought patterns, and challenged how I looked at things. This recurring dream forced me to ask tough questions and revisit a powerful force called "purpose." This dream ignited a fire. I wasn't afraid anymore to be challenged. There was a new excitement to learn, correct and adjust. I was so excited that it could not be contained and held just for me. This had to be passed on and shared.

Chapter 2

(R)elentless

pg.11

Be Real. You must tell yourself the truth to move forward. It starts here. Truth is not always the easiest thing to embrace. To be completely honest, truth can be scary and librating at the same time. For the majority people are not comfortable with their truth because of how they think people will respond and or treat them. If you haven't figured it out, depending on the response or lack of response from people will keep you from true fulfillment. I want to tell you plainly, it is ok to be you. Showing people who you are is ok. I know that they have made you unsafe but it doesn't even matter when it's authentic.

We live in a beautiful age of technology. An age of sharing information that to be is not always true but one could portray it as their truth. One could manipulate information and pictures through technology that could create a certain perception in your mind that life for them is a certain way. So much has gone on in the news, media and the social network that has portrayed and painted people in ways that are not the truth. As beautiful as technology is, it also has proven to be extremely dangerous and detrimental. Just because something is shown and or told to you doesn't mean that it is the truth.

On every social media network the hashtag (#) has become a symbol which captures conversations by subject. The hashtag makes it easy to find every picture and post under that hash tagged subject. It creates a volume of information and images that are not always based in context or truth. This is the ongoing attraction of social media. It allows one to filter through conversations, posts and images that they are not interested in. If not careful this information could be perceived as real/truth. When in fact we are at the mercy of what people tell us and show us. Just because it is told and shown with passion doesn't mean that it's real. This is the danger of measuring your life next to something you see on social media. The house might be an Airbnb, the car might be rented, the jewelry might be borrowed and the vacation might be a promotional giveaway to promote buying a timeshare. Here is the point I could hashtag anything but is it who I am or is it who I am striving to be, or is it what I feel in the moment. There should be more to you than living off a moment.

Time proves the truth. Time exposes what the truth really is. Time reveals truth and gives us a clear look at what things really are. The hard lesson even in marriage the way it was designed and formed was to rid one of anything false, to bring two people to a place of truth.

To say I wanted to write a book was easy, and to be honest it felt good to say it. Putting together a plan and adapting a strategy on how I was going to complete the project was very challenging. (It was relentless in itself.)

Part of what I hope to put forth from this book is that when you receive the strength and confidence to tell yourself the truth, you will also receive the intention and courage to move forward and become what you were created to be. It's easier said than done but it can be done.

Telling yourself the truth is something one has to unfortunately grow into at times. The reason is that at times you don't appreciate and or value the truth about yourself. To see accurately is very valuable. I personally grew to the place where I was ready to tell myself the truth so I could move forward and really be relentless.

I wasn't trying to dig up the past just to dig it up. I wanted to face it. I was looking for the pattern, the reason why I made certain decisions and/or thought a certain way. To be real and honest with yourself requires one to have a desire to get better.

THE CAUTION OR WARNING here is that truth can be difficult to see at times. It is a challenge at times to see certain things about yourself that you have never seen before. It can be very dark and overwhelming to see yourself for the first time.

The benefit is that seeing your truth and or recognizing your mistakes gives you a clear picture of what and how you need to adjust.

This truth doesn't come without investigation. When you work to discover why you made mistakes or why you haven't moved on a project, you find the beginning of understanding. And with understanding of your truth, you will discover the beauty of owning it and taking responsibility.

This investigation can lead to finding people to blame in your life for the things that you have done or the mistakes that you have made. But, what you will see is that blaming people won't lead you to growth.

We tell ourselves the truth to move forward. We do tell ourselves the truth not just to stay where we are and be strong. That's ridiculous. We don't have to stay in the situation that we are in. YOU DON'T HAVE TO LOSE.

And maybe, just maybe, if we investigate we will find out things are not as they seem. Maybe it's perception and not reality. Take a second to look at it, fight the urge to become so frustrated that you're afraid to look at it. Most people get so mad in confrontation that they can't function and communicate.

1. What are they feeling?
2. What is actually wrong?

3. What actually made them mad?

I was very blessed and granted the amazing opportunity to play College Basketball at Xavier University in Cincinnati, Ohio, during the tenure of the late George "Skip" Prosser. I remember how I felt going to a Xavier game as a 6th grader, and watching Brian Grant and Aaron Williams play. I really didn't even know what I was watching, but I know that the love I felt for basketball in those earlier years was so real.

As a high school basketball player, my dream and my goal were always to play basketball beyond high school. I wanted to continue traveling – an experience I believe saved my life.

Being able to travel at 14 to 15 years old really changed my perception of my life, my neighborhood and my worldview at that time. What traveling allowed me to do was to see what my part really was in making my goal of playing college basketball a reality.

On the court I took care of business, but in the classroom that same dedication, hard work and application wasn't applied. I'm not sure why back then I wasn't able to make that transformation. I shared that we tell ourselves to make the adjustment. Making the adjustment is key but not always accessible in how. These three things that I lacked in the classroom but practiced on the

court landed me in a situation where I was faced with a necessary conversation with myself.

It also caused the NCAA to rule me as academically ineligible (so embarrassing and a major problem). The blessed part was that Xavier University was willing to give me an opportunity to prove myself as a student athlete for one year. IF, and it was a big "IF," I proved myself as a student athlete, then the reward was an offer of an athletic scholarship.

Man, that was a very intense but relentless conversation at O'Connor Sports Center (This was three years before the Cintas Center was erected). My mother and father accompanied me to Coach Prosser's office one afternoon to discuss my future.

Coach Prosser sat at his desk, leading the conversation. He laid all the details on the table. My mother and father didn't say much of anything -- maybe a question here and there. Coach Prosser talked about how hard and challenging it would be and all that would be required of me in that first year.

In that room, before Coach Prosser and my parents, I made a conscious decision and a verbal declaration. I was asked, after everything was laid out before me, did I have anything to say or if I had any questions. Not even really knowing the gravity of what was going on, I said "I'm really tired of talking about it, and I'm ready to get to it." I took full responsibility for the actions that lead up to this conversation. Here is where I challenge every student athlete, every coach, every parent of a student athlete that this is a part of the deal. I don't fault any of those individuals that were in my life. The lesson is that you have to work in balance. Eventually if you don't work in balance it will become a part of everything that you do.

Taking responsibility was very crucial to the process of being real and telling myself the truth and seeing the fruit of my honesty to myself. It helped me to:

1. Grow up
2. Reach my goals
3. Stay focused, while balancing personal life along with sports and my studies. (Realizing the necessity of balancing your personal life can make or break being honest with yourself.)

To be relentless and be honest at that point was

me recognizing and admitting that everything I was currently doing in the classroom DID NOT WORK toward reaching those three goals. That was something I had to do. It is something YOU must also do, to tell yourself the truth and not repeat the same bad decisions. The opposite of accepting responsibility is making excuses.

Making excuses takes on an image of making a circle over and over again. Wondering what the use for the rest of the space on the paper is for. Not recognizing the value of more space to move and be creative. My father would often tell me " nobody is going to give you anything". I have understood this statement that it takes on many different forms. Making excuses and blaming other people for things that you have control over reveals something. It reveals that there is fear present. There is something that you don't want to see and or something that you are not ready to deal with. That's not a judgement that extends a hand up because I have been in that place as well.

So, here are the stipulations of my agreement with Xavier University, which I had to shake on and then adhere to. Just because I shook on it doesn't mean I understood what I was doing because I didn't. Nor did I have a strategy to not repeat my academic performance that I put forth in High School.

I was declared a partial qualifier as a student/athlete. I could not practice nor could I travel with the team for the entirety of my freshman year, and I could not stay on campus.

I agreed to these stipulations, but during that first year I felt overwhelmingly uncomfortable and I seemed to be out of place. I felt weird and I'm sure I equally came off that way. But here was the opportunity that I was sure that I would receive to play basketball. I honestly have to say that I couldn't focus clearly at first. Sitting out of basketball that one year caused a bit of a distraction. Completely unfocused, embarrassed and so many other feelings that I could not manage. As I set out I started working at a 5 star restaurant downtown Cincinnati, Ohio in the Omni Hilton Hotel. I was a part-time busboy at night and a Xavier student athlete during the day. Bussing tables was a very humbling experience that I will never forget. I think it taught me that no matter the big goal that you have to be willing to do the dirty work. For an entire year I would catch the bus down to the Omni Hilton Hotel, wearing dress pants, dress shoes with a tie and bus tables. I daydreamed a lot and focused on not dropping any dish or food. For the first time in almost 10 years I didn't have a basketball season to prepare for. There was no conditioning that I had to dread but looked forward to. It was an awkward year all the way around. I was 19 years old and the cycle and familiarity of basketball was not there. I didn't want to get used to the absence of basketball.

Basketball gave me identity and it gave me self-confidence. It built a habit in me that gave me hope to exist and now this inspiration was gone when I needed it the most – or so it seemed.

I felt I needed the inspiration to prove that I was a student athlete. But in the midst of all of that, I had to ask myself a question: "Do I have what it takes to be successful in the classroom?" With my academic history in mind I entered the college classroom very intimidated. Unsure of myself academically, athletically still in a shock that I had to sit out for the year. But the relentless questions started to happen.

You see, here is where the change into being relentless happens, when you start asking yourself the tough questions. That's what I had to do. What I discovered in asking that tough question was that it helped me begin to change my perspective.

Perspective is a powerful thing that can determine a lot. And if you are not careful, you will base life altering situations on your perspectives that are jaded – lacking enthusiasm or boring. They may be jaded because of things that haven't been properly processed and challenged by these real questions.

PERCEPTION vs REALITY

What is Real? What is just perspective? Maybe reality is not that bad? Maybe there is something useful and life changing that telling the truth when surfaced would be helpful and beneficial. What is there to learn from this? Uncomfortable and unsure should lead to discovery.

I learned a very interesting lesson on the difference between reality and perspective. If you are going to be RELENTLESS in every area of your life, it is crucial that you learn the difference.

The reason it's crucial is that if you operate your life primarily off of perspective, then your life will be filled with horrible decisions based on a jaded perspective.

Teachable Moments of Life

Mirror, Mirror on the Wall

It's very easy to go through a moment of life, and see yourself dangle between low self-esteem and insecurity. Finally being real with yourself can be very dark and very scary. But, truth is needed for you to grow. Growth will not happen if you don't work to get to your truth.

Between 2003 and 2004, I worked for a county family service agency. It really was an awesome training place for me. I learned how to deal with crisis, deal with families, identify a problem and create a quick and workable solution.

One particular situation sticks out to me. I was called out to the daycare of one of the kids on my caseload. I was called out to a location about 30 to 40 minutes away because there was the

potential of substantial physical abuse – in other words, A MESS.

A report of abuse normally comes from the school, daycare, after school program or other places where children are cared for. This particular situation already had a red flag and it was very sensitive.

My immediate supervisor rode with me to the daycare. During the ride we went over the last time I saw the child. By the time we got there, there were a total of six professionals there to examine this child. But the child didn't seem to be phased.

We all stood around scratching our heads, trying to figure out how this bruise on the child's back was so bad, but the child did not show any other sign of emotional upset or physical trauma.

After several minutes of this, another nurse comes into the room. So, now there is one county sheriff, one county caseworker, one county clinical supervisor, one daycare worker, one day care supervisor all there to look at the bruise and assess the situation.

The nurse comes in, takes one look at the child and the bruise and leaves. Minutes later she comes back in with a warm soapy towel and wipes the back of the child clean. The report is that the child had been playing in paint and it dried.

Wow!!!! Just paint? Really? Everyone in the room breathed a sigh of relief. But, the initial perception was that the child was abused, and that it didn't look good for the parents. If there had been actual abuse, there had to be an investigation and the child would be removed again until we came to some conclusion. Like I said, it would have been a mess!

Imagine what would have happened if we hadn't investigated further – if we hadn't challenged our perception in the situation and established the reality.

As silly and obvious as that sounds, people, including me, live their life that way. They live a life of perception and never really get to the base of what is true.

You cannot make a sound decision based on perception of something or someone. You are going to end up making a mistake. Do me a favor. Take a deep breath and tell yourself the truth.

Chapter 3

R(e)lentless

pg.25

Evaluate (verb) - form an idea of the amount, number, or value of; assess. In Mathematics - find a numerical expression or equivalent for (equation, formula, or function).

When I fell in love with basketball, I mean I fell in love with everything about it! I can remember that feeling and that smell of the heat and gym floor wax mix. I remember coming in from outside, knocking the snow off my shoes and taking off my big heavy coat, laughing and talking with teammates about the last game. We were teasing each other about stuff that went on in the last game, talking about our favorite professional team and favorite player.

The traveling and the excitement drove me and caused me to daydream about the upcoming game. I have to admit that playing basketball and being part of a team and having that to look forward to each season saved my life. It gave me something to hope for and to push towards.

Hope helps give you the ability to focus. Hope gives you something to look for and a supernatural push, to keep going when you want to quit. Being on a team creates a new world for a person and gives you such a great sense of belonging. I benefited so much from being on a team, learning from different people, going to their house, meeting their family. A team is social and it develops social skills and relationships that last forever. There is always a good story to tell when teammates get together. People that have competed and been on teams grow up to be the best employees. I actually got a job on the strength the person hiring played in college and he understood the advantage a former teammate has coming into any place of business. The advantage is there is an understanding of teamwork, goals, playing your role and understanding your role as it relates to the overall team's success.

I grew up playing basketball in a very competitive environment. There were so many games, so many gyms, I probably ran up and down a basketball court a million times. Out of all the things that I was blessed by basketball to experience, being in the game and the different situations I encountered taught me the most. The different possessions in the very intense moments that never called for overreacting. Those moments taught that leaning on your preparations and training produced a winning outcome.

As I have gotten older I have learned so much from the privilege of taking a "time out." Within a game each team has so many full timeouts (1 minute) and so many 30 second timeouts. So much can be done with so little time.

I never really fully appreciated the time out. I guess maybe I only thought about it as a cheat way to catch my breath and grab a quick drink. In an intense game, where the score is tied and or even when the score is against you, a time out is essentially there so that you can evaluate the situation and make an adjustment.

The most challenging part about making an adjustment in such a fast paced game, is that time is short. So, since the time frame that you have to decide on is short, it's crucial to quickly identify what's going on and adjust according to the outcome that you want.

So, you have to be:

1. As fast as you can, **identify** the issue that is keeping you from your desired outcome. 2. Make an adjustment based upon what you see as the problem.
3. Have a clear understanding of how to execute the adjustment.

All of this has to be done before the whistle blows. What the game I fell in love with taught me was that you have to make an adjustment and you must be brave enough to identify the issue that is keeping you from your goal.

It's the same in life as it is in a basketball game, when emotions flare, adrenaline is moving crazy, people are creating a noise, and you must make an adjustment in this very chaotic, hostile environment.

Identify - establish or indicate who or what (someone or something) is. Associate (someone) closely with; regard (someone) as having strong links with.

I started asking myself questions about what I understood about timeouts.
Question #1 is: Once I identify the problem, exactly what do I need to adjust? (It could be very possible that not everything needs to be adjusted.)

Question #2 is: If everybody has the same amount of time during the game, why can't better adjustments be made?

Question #3 is: What factors contribute to errors in adjusting? Is it the pressure? Is it the environment or the noise around you? Is it the presence of possible defeat or failure?

What I discovered is that evaluating and making the adjustments needed becomes an action that says I am taking advantage of the time given to me to correct my behavior.

We all have a purpose. Some identify it sooner than others. There is a journey all of us go through to reach or fulfill our purpose. Along the way you have to be so relentless that you identify behaviors and things that do help you stretch and reach your goal. I encourage you to summon the courage to reach out and make the adjustment.

The best basketball coaches in the world pride themselves on the preparation that they have put forth and their ability to make game time adjustments.

The adjustments they make are based on what they can identify going against the team objective. No matter what, they hold onto the goal and stand ready to call a "time out" if they need to adjust to correct something.

Make sure you evaluate where you are, because your future depends on it. Evaluate your daily activities to make sure they match up to your overall goal.

If you need to take a time out to make the adjustment, based on what you have evaluated, TAKE SOME TIME. There is no shame in being down 5 and taking a time out, only to come back and win by 20.

You would celebrate the opportunity to take that

time out and adjust. If you need to make a second adjustment to reach your goal, that's fine too. It shows you are beginning to start living on purpose. As you learn to evaluate and identify the issues standing in your way, now you prepare different approaches. Each situation is handled differently, based on the evaluation.

BACK TO BASKETBALL

A part of basketball is training and practicing. The training develops your body, both to get stronger and to condition you for what is required. If you fail to properly train, you will be on the team but you will not do well. You have to prepare, once you evaluate and see what it takes to succeed.

Though I fought for and eventually earned an athletic scholarship, I did not contribute on the court the way I hoped and desired.

Of course, I was behind because I sat out a year. But the greater issue was what I was doing with the time I had, during the year I sat out. My lack of preparation was revealed once I stepped on the court.

I remember being called out by a teammate at Xavier University (this teammate went on to be an NBA Allstar and NBA champion) during summer workout. I believe he had become very concerned about why I wasn't playing.

He had watched me dominate practices as a scout team player, so he talked with the coaches on my behalf.

One day during open gym, he sat out that day while the rest of us were playing. During a transition between offense to defense in the practice session, he yelled to me, "Mac, this is why you don't play."

Essentially, he was saying I hadn't put forth the work in my training. Therefore the coaches couldn't trust me, because I wasn't prepared for success. It was so true. I was more concerned with making excuses. "Failing to prepare is preparing to fail."

Chapter 4
Re(L)entless

pg.32

Coach Skip Prosser would say to all of us at Xavier University: "Failing to prepare is preparing to fail."

Love – an intense feeling of deep affection.

It's an interesting definition for a word that is thrown around so carelessly, in every way possible. To say that you love something or love someone is easy.

I really think that when you say "I love you" to someone you really can mean it, at that time. Words do have power, but although you love something and say you love something, it doesn't mean you always understand what is involved in loving the object of your affection. This concept of Love has to be taught in order to help people preserve what they hold near.

To say you love something is very important in pursuing your passion. What needs to follow is real conversation around what that means and what that looks like on a daily basis.

From that conversation about what you love and why you love what you say you love, should come a clear strategy. Somewhere along the line the confession of love should convict you to grow in what you love. That should be the approach every day.

IS IT LOVE OR IS IT LIKE?

Two people meet each other and make a decision to spend time with each other. As they make a decision to spend time with one another, they start to share intimate things about each other that bring them closer and cause them to realize that they want to be together. In the process of getting to know each other, they fall in love.

I never really, fully understood why we say "fall in love." It really should be "grow into love," and from this feeling of deep affection, love is then conceived.

The feeling of loving something is great. Food seems to taste better, holidays seem to have more fulfillment. Where the feeling of love begins to lose its taste is when adversity hits and the commitment is questioned and put to the test.

See, it is easy for someone to say out of their mouth they love someone or something. It's easy to say that because there is no commitment attached. I really believe that if there was a way to somehow immediately feel the heaviness of the commitment of what you say when you say "you love," you would watch what you say.

I can remember dreaming of having a dog. I would fantasize about the time we would spend together, and the games that the dog and I would play.

That feeling was amazing but it only lasted until the first night when I had to wake up out of a dead sleep and take the dog outside to use the restroom. I remember the weight of that responsibility, when I wanted to go out of town but couldn't.

When you truly love something and really want that something to be in your life forever, there must be commitment -- strong, lasting commitment.

This level of commitment doesn't come easy and it for sure doesn't only come from your mouth, but also from your heart and your mind (your level of understanding). I learned this lesson very early on in life and my hope is that I clearly communicate it to you so that you can apply it in your personal life.

Playing basketball taught me how to be

committed. Not saying I was always committed, but it also taught me what happens when you say you love something and you're not committed. If you are not committed to it and willing to sacrifice for it, doing whatever it calls for, YOU DON'T LOVE IT, YOU LIKE IT.

Love and sacrifice go hand in hand.

COMMITMENT

Commitment - the state or quality of being dedicated to a cause, activity, a pledge or undertaking.

The ideal of achieving something feels so good and it is so exciting. But, the heaviness of the commitment that it takes to actually achieve it is not always realized.

The use of the word love can't be used loosely. Failure to realize the serious commitment that is behind the word creates a frustration that is overwhelming.

Commitment separates people into different groups. Group One are those who make you question their love commitment. Whether it's a marriage, another educational degree or a new job, when what they love becomes frustrating they begin to question whether they really love it enough to stay and/or keep loving it.

WHAT HAPPENED? You were so in love, so infatuated with the ideal of it. But, you never sat down and considered the commitment it would take to maintain this love and move it more aggressively forward. You also never figured out a strategy on how to handle things when it stopped feeling good. This is what you have to plan for – what to do when what you say you love is challenged by frustration and mismanaged expectation.

I am not telling you to stop dreaming so big, but what I am saying is that as your dream progresses, let a strategy to deal with boredom and dissatisfaction be a part of the dreams. Know that frustration and adversity WILL come.

As you dream, let the preparation of what will be the game plan when adversity hits and your love is tried. When your love for something is tried, let commitment stand up for a while until the love for it is strong enough to stand up again.

Most people make a dangerous move and quit when their love is frustrated. This is not wise, nor will it move you forward. Let the love sit for a second and let the commitment be strong enough to see it through to completion.

All you must do is to keep getting up every day. Keep moving. When frustration comes in, refocus your passion with commitment. The day after day grind has to build up for you to actually complete your goal.

This is the question that you have to ask yourself in reference to the big goal: After I have identified what I love, how am I going to piece my days together so that they look like my goal?

Understand that time is not going to wait. The days will turn into weeks, the weeks will turn into months, the months will turn into years. That's a substantiated fact.

As time moves on, there is an expectation that things should not only get older but mature and grow. What is even more frustrating is when time moves on things get older but it never matures. THIS CAN'T BE. Don't lose your love for it just because you were afraid to let your commitment stand.

More Lessons From Basketball

Playing basketball, being on a team, traveling and being a student athlete provided some amazing insight into loving something and having commitment.

There were a lot of things that can happened in a basketball season. A lot happens in a basketball season as a student athlete. The first thing that is obvious is the change of weather that happens within the basketball season.

Most basketball programs begin their season a month after the last game is played, with spring workout (weight lifting and open gym.) Then, after the school year is over there are summer workouts, then preseason workouts that pick up in October.

That's a big time commitment for just saying that you want to play basketball. It challenges how much you mean what you say. With the weather changing in the midst of all, your love for the game becomes challenging.

You have to dress differently going to practice than when you're going to games. This can be a challenge, if you don't have a large, varied wardrobe.
But, what was most challenging for me was that while basketball season was going on other students were doing things and having fun, which I could not be a part of because of my commitment. And if I wanted to continue doing what I loved, I had to sacrifice and stay committed, no matter how I felt.

You never can get in the counter-productive habit of allowing your feelings to stop you from keeping your commitment. Protect your love of it with your commitment to it.

Chapter 5

Rel(e)ntless

pg.39

Educate (Do Your Homework)

Educate:
1. to develop the faculties and powers of (a person) by teaching, instruction, or schooling.
2.qualify by instruction or training for a particular calling, practice, to provide schooling or training; send to school.

Insanity is wasting your life as nothing when you have the blood of a winner flowing in your veins. Insanity is being abused and used, beat down, coasting through life when you have a caged lion locked inside of you. I say, let the God given desire and purpose loose and become relentless. Here is the key to release it.

During the fall seasons of 1994 to 1998, I attended Roger Bacon High School in Cincinnati, Ohio. In the school's administrative wing there was a framed saying that read, "I wish life's problems came to me when I was young and thought I knew everything."

It's an interesting quote, which I have always

thought about -- even more as time has moved on from that moment of being in high school. Throughout my time as a student athlete, which was pretty much the most of my life up to age 21, I never discovered and mastered my learning style – the best way for me to process information, remember facts and understand them.

Most of the time I tried to remember information without completely understanding it. That's a dangerous, ineffective approach to school and any learning environment.

A learning environment is a huge category, because it goes beyond the school building. The opportunity to learn is everywhere and I never realized it. That opportunity is everywhere, and as you grow older, the lessons become universal.

The opportunity to learn is also available even in what could be considered a failure. I tried to stay away from those moments of failure and disappointment, because they brought on emotions that I didn't always know how to manage.

But what I began to develop in my mind's eye was a picture of what I shouldn't do and what I should do. Your whole life becomes a classroom. Everything that happens in it becomes an opportunity to get better, grow and mature. Everything is a pretty big and bold word to use here considering everything you have been through and everything that you have encountered. Think about the most painful and embarrassing thing that you have ever experienced. What was embarrassing about it? Was something said that you didn't like? What about what happened scares you to have people to know? You might miss an opportunity here to grow and understand something you never had an understanding on.

But if you walk around not willing to do the work to understand, you won't grow nor get better. I began to realize that while I was in school, I was being prepared for the world. That included: getting to school on time, the requirements for the dress code, all of it. It was preparation for the world. Preparation is the underlining key to lasting success.

Do the homework. And what you will find is that behind a bunch of seemingly meaningless things there is an education waiting for you, an opportunity for you to look at everything around as a step-up for your future.

Certain things that will be or already are on your personal resume presents a certain message to the world of where you have been, what you know and what you can do.

1. A good education opens your eyes and helps you see what is real and what is true. 2.

A good education makes you better.
3. A good education does not feel good while it is working on you.

I hated homework. It seemed to be a waste of time and seemed to cut into my afternoon life once the school day was done. It is like school was following me home and I didn't want the work or school to know where I lived.

I didn't understand what the homework was given for. And when you don't understand nor trust what is presented before you, it's impossible to buy in to allow it to work.

Question 1 that you should ask yourself during or after each experience is: What did I learn or what can I learn from this?

Beyond the measurements of a physical classroom, your intellect can be enhanced, if you're not too distracted and if you're willing to pay attention.

Then ask yourself Question 2: How can I use the information that I am receiving to make my life better?

Here is where being able to understand the information comes into play. If you work to understand it you can use it to better yourself. If you don't take the time to understand it, if you can't use it you won't see the value of having it in the first place.

When I was in 6th grade the first time I went to Clifton Elementary School in Cincinnati, Ohio. I was the top dog because I was the tallest kid in the 6th.

Academically, I was OK. I was in the school band -- playing the drums, of course -- so I was involved in school activities. If I struggled in the classroom, it was because of my behavior.

Clifton only went to the 6th grade, so when I graduated my parents had to look for another school. The issue was that I had gotten into a bad habit of being lazy in the classroom, so sending me to the public junior high was not an option.

I had to be challenged or I wouldn't have learned anything. So, they enrolled me into a private school, with uniforms, ties, tucked in shirts, the whole nine.

The only issue with starting this new school was that I had to take a placement test. A placement test allowed the school to see where I was academically and what I needed to work on to be successful in their learning community.

Even though I graduated from the 6th grade at Clifton, my placement test scores at Corryville Catholic were low. With the test scores being low, the school suggested I redo the 6th grade again. I wasn't happy at first, and I was even a little embarrassed. But what I soon recognized was that the second time around I understood the information and I therefore was able to use it to my benefit. The ability to push past embarrassment, focus in and take advantage of what was presented to me, was a great opportunity. I learned that education can make you a better person, inside and outside the classroom.

Chapter 6

Rele(n)tless

Notorious -widely and unfavorably known; publicly or generally known, as for a a particular trait.

By the time I started competing in basketball I already had the competitive drive to play and win. I was fortunate in the area of athletics to have two athletic parents.

My mother was a state recognized track and field athlete and my father was a college football player. My mother's brother was an all-state and college football player who was more like my older brother than my uncle. I used to spend summers, weekends and Christmas breaks playing basketball with his friends and teammates.

I played for fun and fun only. I wanted to win but at that age I didn't know how to actually win. Honestly, I didn't understand how to win. Looking back, I wasn't doing enough to chase the win down. My pattern of play was off, and I was too predictable on the court, and my habits needed to change. The habits that I had on the court weren't producing the results that I wanted. Here is the key to pursuing goals and your purpose. When pursuing anything, you have to make sure that your daily habits match what you're trying to pursue. The words notorious and infamous generally carry a negative connotation.

It's consistency that we are after. What is the character trait you want to be known for? What is the habit you have that matches what you are focusing on and or what you want to do? Don't be notorious for "talking a good game" and talking about your big goals, but your daily habits show you're not really serious.

SCOUTING REPORT

What we know is the big goal. It can at times seem so massive, intimidating, unobtainable and bigger than you.

Here is something that might help…

Get a piece of paper and draw a big circle, in the middle of the page. In the circle write what you feel is the main thing that you want to do in life. So for example I did this exercise and inside of my circle I put " help people, inspire people and motivate people to be who they were created to be". So now that you have your circle filled in, draw about 5 lines pointing out from the circle. On the 5 lines list what that looks like to you in 5 different ways. For example , one of my lines had an author on it even before I was a published author. What this exercise is working to do is jump start your imagination and create a daily checklist within a big vision. This is creating a strategy that you can see and begin to implement your big goal each day. This will keep you moving and working towards the big goal.

A LESSON FROM SOCIAL MEDIA

We live in the social media age and I absolutely love it because I get and understand social media. Those that hate social media and think it's bad for the next generation simply do not understand it. I would always caution you to work to get understanding before you make judgement on anything. When you don't understand it you don't have the capacity to make it work for you. Social media has made it easy for the world to connect, that is the summary of its ability. There is freedom that social media gives each individual that is logged in. Social media also allows one to create a fantasy as well. These two components of social media are strong and if mishandled in any way it becomes dangerous, making more problems than giving you the advantage. The third component of social media is responsibility. This component of social media allows you to benefit from the freedom and the fantasy that it was created to give. If you can be responsible enough with the freedom you can create a space of major influence.

With the power of connecting people that would not be able to get to each other on social media, it has created the ability to create fantasy about who you really are. One could post a picture with a certain angle and lighting that projects a lifestyle that they are not really living. When you post a picture on social media we all become at the mercy of what your caption is. Very powerful ability that comes from a picture but it works.

Years ago that's not how pictures were viewed by people. In order to view pictures of family and close friends you would actually have to schedule a time and place to view new pictures. To hear the caption of those pictures was a sign that you have a relationship with those who own the pictures. With social media you can control the narrative of your life without people really knowing who you really are. You can create a habit, a resume about what you aspire to be and don't have to be that person.

So many people have been fooled by this simple freedom that we all have to create a narrative. You control your narrative and that's freedom and power. Now that you know you have freedom and power to control your narrative, use it to your advantage. This is your responsibility to understand your freedom and use it. Just being free is not enough. To be free and to use your freedom to the advantage of advancing life around is the responsibility of all humanity.

Notorious is a reputation built on what we know about you, based on a daily consistency of not following through.

Behavior is the way we communicate nonverbally. It is the consistency of actions that produce something either of value or notice. The old saying is: "Actions speak louder than words."

How do I reach my goal or the goal that has been set before me? I begin to change my consistency of habit. In small increments I change. Find a way to challenge every negative thought, every negative behavior and make them conform to what's needed to match your goal.

What is it that you are known for? Do you like what you are known for and does it match what you are going after? Are your habits lining up to become what helps you reach your goal and fulfill your purpose? If your habits do not daily lead you to fulfill your goal then your habits need to change.

What are habits? And how are they formed? Is it something that we are born with? How do you change bad habits and turn them into good habits that are daily steps that build, discipline and carry you to your goal? These are tough questions that nobody wants to ask themselves.

But then again, why wouldn't you ask yourself these questions if you are really serious about your goal? I believe what happens in all of us initially is that self-defending, self-preserving system called pride.

This self-defeating system causes us to protect our feelings, at times to sabotage ourselves, if we let it. But, YOU HAVE TO ASK YOURSELF THESE QUESTIONS. I have to tell you here where the model of being relentless is placed to help because right here you have to challenge yourself. You have to fight against yourself which is not always easy. To go against the grain of your own built in defense mechanism is like in a boxing match against you. To see yourself for the first time is intimidating but to see your destructive patterns for the first time is even scary. These questions have to be asked and you cannot be afraid of yourself.

It's imperative to who you are and what you're made up of, to build habits that will create your personal brand. To build a notorious habit is to have a personal significant fingerprint that identifies you to the world.

This is what you're known for by your fingerprint and your brand. You have a brand and you were born to give it to the world. Everybody is born with a fingerprint, it's what you were born with. Since we were all born with a fingerprint then there are habits that we all have. We have habits that make us who we are. The problem is there are habits that we have that do not help us achieve anything.

If we become comfortable with those habits that cause us not to reach what we were created to do, we have to do something about that. We have to eliminate them. Then there are habits that we need to have that are not a part of our daily routine and our daily focus, which we should practice. You could spend your whole life saying what you want but not willing to make the change and or adjustment to be on the path to obtain it.

It may seem strange to say it, but you have to be notorious. You have to be so willing to stick to your habit or stick to the course that the habit will lead you to, until you reach your destination.

Your brand, your fingerprint is who you were created to be. Being notorious takes a mature level of understanding. I want to share something very crucial with you. There is a force that wants to strip you of this fingerprint and tear you away from this consistency, and make you like everybody else. You have to fight to protect your fingerprint because there is something that you have that the world needs. If you settle and devalue your fingerprint we will never get what you were born to give to the work. Fight the urge to settle not to be who you were created to be.

THERE CAN BE NO CUTTING CORNERS.

It has to be a relentless drive, almost an obsession, for you to succeed. Obsess it down to every single detail, every simple detail. Look at it, pay attention to it. Truth is in the details.
There is a saying in competitive sports that you can't cheat the game. And if you try to cheat the game, you will quickly understand that truth (whatever the game is.).

The game will quickly teach you and expose you for what you did not do or what you did that did not work in advance towards making you successful.

It is as simple as to run sprints after practice and not touch the line. But you come close enough, just close enough for the coach to see but you never really touch the line.

This is habit forming, psychologically producing something in you called a habit. This particular habit is not finishing things to the end. This is spending your energy, trying to make it easy on yourself and not seeing the success in the end.

It is the sacrifice of doing what is right when nobody's looking. This produces a habit. What happens with this particular habit is that you get to the game and you don't have a habit of quitting or doubting. The habit that you have created is a habit to find a reason to keep going.

Having a habit to get tough when it stops being fun, that you are willing to pay the sacrifice, is the key to success.

Successful habits make it or break it. The success is in the preparation.

Daily Habits
Consistency>Discipline>Your Goal

We don't want to hear your excuses when the plan doesn't work. Make the adjustments. Look at your daily goal. Let your daily routine match the overall goal. When your daily habits match what the overall goal is, you will achieve it.

How do you build consistency? Change starts when you realize the issues that kept you from being successful in the past. After you come to accept these truths about yourself and set short term goals, you will see that they are really big goal achievements in the making.

First, is the realization that you have to implement those steps that are correct whether it produces right away or not.

For example: When you are shooting a basketball properly, the form is
   1. One hand on the side of the basketball and

your writing or dominant hand at the center. 2. Shoulders square, lined up to the basket. 3. Feet balanced, shoulder length apart, locked on the basket.
4. When releasing the ball, you keep your eyes focused on the basket.
5. Release the ball at the top of your jump.
6. Hold the follow through.

Now even though this is the correct form and protocol for the ball to go in, you have to repeat this and practice this until these steps become a skill set that is memorized to your muscle memory. Once you realize and implement, you still have to repeat it. And this is how you actively build consistency.

REALIZE>IMPLEMENT>REPETITION

These steps build the reputation. Not from the heart of wanting attention from people but from the desire to build consistency and discipline. This is a relentless behavior to develop.

Chapter 7

Relen(T)less

pg.55

Temperature- a measure of the warmth or coldness of an object or substance with reference to some standard value. The temperature of two systems is the same when the systems are in thermal equilibrium.

I believe in the power of seasons. I believe that in the seasons we experience through the calendar year we have the opportunity to make adjustments, sow, work what we have sown, and reap the harvest.

To everything there is a season, and a **time** to every purpose under heaven. Time becomes key. Time becomes a very beautiful friend. One should appreciate time, because in time what you were created to do will come to pass. Time is on your side. Everything that you are supposed to do, you will do. There is a self inflicted pressure that exist when you

Would you rather…
Cut a piece of wood 10 times and get it right the last time that you cut? Or measure 10 times, cut once and get it right? It would be best practice to measure 10 times and cut once. It may be

tough, uncomfortable and time consuming but it is effective and efficient.

It is relentless, and allows you to reach your goal, if you measure and then do the following: 1. Make the decision.
   2. Move forward on anything.
   3. Quit or stay put.
   4. Begin something.

When you take the time and measure, it allows you the ability to weigh all the options and to see them clearly. Measuring shows how to cut and where to cut it properly. Measuring restrains the compulsion to just cut it to get it done.

Most rush to do and not take their time to get it done right. Measure it, and weigh it with care. And once you take your time and consider all angles, CUT IT.

I wondered why one would choose to cut without first measuring it out. When you don't measure it's impossible to really know what you have. If you don't measure and know what you really have, then it's impossible to know how to fully use what you've got.

This is where most people stay -- living in regret, wishing that they had done something different, planned better, asked more questions, taken better advantage of the opportunity. Usually when someone rushes to make a cut, it's because feelings are involved with it and feelings will always cloud judgment. Feelings involved in making these decisions cause you to react to a situation instead of moving wisely through the situation.

This is dealing with what everybody in the world has to deal with. It is called life. You have to sit back at times, come out of your feelings, measure and move forward with the focus that this next decision could affect the rest of your life.

Slow down. Would you rather slow down and make the right cut now or spend years dealing with a hacked-up decision that you have to fix for life? Cutting or making this decision is going to take some time. This cut is going to take some patience and some research. Some questions need to be asked, in order to cut precisely.

When I was at Xavier I struggled at first because my awareness of the situation was off and I didn't fully take advantage. It wasn't until later on that I somewhat realized the situation. The ability to take full advantage of a situation while you're in the situation is a super power. Not only is it a super power it is gaining the advantage.

A Cautionary Tale
Here is a story and the lesson about what happens when you are in your feelings and you rush to cut 10 times instead of measuring 10 times and then cutting once. The beauty of

walking on to Xavier's basketball team as a partial qualifier is that once you prove yourself as a student the first year, you still get four years to earn your Bachelor's degree.

Once I stopped feeling sorry for myself, I began to realize the opportunities in front of me. You can be so in your feelings that it almost blinds you from seeing the opportunities ahead of you and around you. That is a very dangerous place to be – being in your feelings while attempting to make decisions.

It never comes out right and making decisions from your feelings will always result in immediate satisfaction but it can lead to long term regret. Making decisions from your feelings will always result in a quick fix but years of damage. And sometimes the damage doesn't reveal itself until some time has passed.

I did not play like I wanted to at Xavier University, but I got what I really came for -- which was a degree. I received a Bachelor of Science in Criminal Justice. My reasoning for that degree was to originally become a probation officer. I thought at the time it would be cool to be a probation officer.

Because I didn't play as much as I wanted to, I was in my feelings. I admit that it took a long time to get out of my feelings, primarily because I was being defensive about why I didn't play.

The whole thing made me uncomfortable and embarrassed. What I recognize now is that you can spend years blaming everything and everybody but you for your situation. That's a very dark, confused place to be.

I NEVER WANT TO GO BACK into my feelings so much that I'm blind. I was in my feelings and made a decision while I was there. Though I got my degree, I could have stayed at Xavier and enrolled into the Master's degree program and stayed on the team.

See this is where the lack of taking the temperature of the situation comes into play. While in your feelings you cannot make sound decisions. Being in your feelings will cost you time, money, relationships and so much more.

Chapter 8

Relent(L)ess

pg.60

Live – to practice, represent or exhibit in one's behavior

To live your brand is really a mental commitment to who you are. Out of all the things you can be in the world of possibilities, you have to commit to it and wear it in your behavior. This is true across the board.

If you cannot wear it in your behavior, where people can see it physically on you, then it's not believable. The issue with just saying it and just talking about it is that it's just a loose thought that's not attached securely to any solid commitment. If you want to see it, live it and attach it to a commitment.

By the time that sophomore year rolled around at Xavier, I was overweight and completely out of shape. I wasted a year, sitting out and feeling sorry for myself. For an entire basketball season, I refused to wear my love for basketball and my desire for success in my behavior. My self pity got completely out of control and it showed.

My commitment was nowhere to be found. With no commitment, you will not behave in the direction of your goals. Not playing that first year and living at home with my parents was a daily reminder of my lack of mental commitment.

I had to get out of my feelings. You have to come out of your feelings in order to achieve your goals and live your dream. The challenge is being able to see some aspect of growth and forward movement that motivates you daily.

I realized that everything that seemed to be insignificant and small in relation to my overall goal was, in fact, significant.

Where was my error? Where was the mental adjustment needed? Where was my perspective off, so far off that it affected the lack of follow-through in my behavior?

I can remember being so uncomfortable, so out of place and embarrassed when I came around the rest of the team that was actually playing.

What could I do about that? Do I stay in my feelings? Do I try to change and go to another school? Was it me? Was it them? It was easy to linger in blame and make many excuses. It could be very comfortable there.

But what I clearly began to understand was that

living in excuses and blaming other people would never help me or anybody else reach their goal. If the mind is transformed, trust and believe that the behavior will follow. Little by little, with conscious effort and commitment, daily behavior will change and you will live out your vision.

You cannot be afraid to live! It sounds simple, but it's not. It's possible for you to live your life to the fullest, but it's going to take a different daily practice in order to get there.

Finally, I made a decision. I was going to do whatever I needed to do to graduate early. It was so out of reach, but I wanted it so bad. I was out to prove a point.

I didn't play as I felt I should have, and I was tired of being upset over it. I wanted to play, and I wanted to be a part of the team's success. At the time, I felt that being on the floor was the only way to share in the team's success.

I felt dismissed from the team, the game, the coaches etc. What did I possibly have to inspire me to behave differently? What could I look at to pull myself closer to feeling a part of the team?

I wanted to be connected. I wanted to grab hold of something in order to feel alive. I wanted to be controlled by my purpose and destiny, not by my emotions that can be all over the place. My goals became simple.

I decided: If they won't put me into the game, I'm going to be extremely competitive in practice and have fun because I'm playing hard. I'm going to be the best teammate in the locker room, on the bench, in the airport, in the hotel and in the classroom.

I'm going to be the best student athlete, figuring out a way to complete every assignment on time, go to every class and do all of it with a smile. I would go to the gym late at night and play shooting games with one of the team managers, just to get up shots. I was living it. I was wearing it. And it felt great!!!!

I was no longer controlled by what I couldn't control. I was now being controlled by my purpose. And once I identified my purpose, my behavior changed.

This is living controlled by purpose -- living with your eyes on where you are headed.

Chapter 9

Relentl(e)ss

Excite - to cause; awaken

Here's how to take hold of Transferable energy, Marketable energy.

I'll begin with the story of going to my Uncle's football game and the energy that I felt to be an athlete.

If I believe it, if I want it, and if I wear it in my behavior, then it should in some way inspire somebody else.

My mom is one of 11 children, 10 girls and 1 boy who is the baby. My mom tells the story that there was a period of time when my grandmother was always pregnant. How tough my grandmother was to carry 11 people inside of her. 11 people with different personalities but similar characteristics. I had 10 aunts and one uncle. MAN!!! A big family is so much fun and you learn so much pertaining to being able to effectively socialize with the rest of the world through your family. You learn how to communicate, handle conflict, pursue your purpose or make excuses, your choice of mate, your decision making at the dinner table whether healthy or unhealthy it all comes from what you see within your family.

Can you imagine what our family gatherings look like? There were usually more people than there was space, which presents problems of its own. There are many dynamics to a family that size, as you would assume.

But, there is a lot of strength that comes from being a part of a large family too. I recognize that it really is a blessing to be from a family that size. You have so many personalities and so many different interests.

One of things that can happen in a family that size is that if the family isn't careful, more attention is paid to this person than to that person. That's a very real and damaging dynamic, especially as the family grows. The measurement of success can be altered and/or catered to a particular person or persons, if the family is not careful. Most grew up in a big family and because of these dynamics that I just named no longer care to be around their family.

It seems simple, but your family becomes your world, a community in itself, a sub-culture even. And if you feel as if your family doesn't accept you or doesn't support you, it can cause internal and lasting damage. So, these dynamics can make or break you. It's interesting who it makes and who it breaks, who it pushes and who it subconsciously crushes. Think about how you grow up with the same conditions and same DNA, same potential to become what you were created to be.

When my grandfather and grandmother started having kids, they ended up with two different sets – an older set and a younger set.

Both of my grandparents were born and raised in Huntsville, Alabama with humble beginnings. My two older aunts were actually born in Alabama too. But, when my grandfather moved to Ohio for work and a better life for his family, my two older aunts were left behind.

I celebrate my grandfather, because it took incredible courage and faith to make a major move like that. This man became a perfect picture of relentlessness to all of us. My grandmother had that same spirit of tenacity. to leave home and chase down a better life. It takes this tenacity to leap at a better life and go against the grain to chase down purpose. Most importantly open the doors to greater and bigger opportunities. That takes courage, vision and a strategy to achieve.

The two different sets of children are famously known as the "Big Guys" and the "Little Guys." My mom is a part of the big guys. Because there were so many kids in the house at one time, the big guys would help raise and care for the little guys. There was a five year difference between my aunt, who is the baby of the older guys, and my aunt who is the eldest of the younger guys. There are five girls that make up the older guys and five girls and one boy that make up the younger guys.

Can you imagine just one boy in the midst of 10 girls? And that's not to mention my older aunts were adults in their 20s and 30s by the time my uncle came along. He essentially had 11 mothers.

Though the dynamics in a big family are many, one of the dynamics I personally benefited from and enjoyed was to have an uncle close to my age. My uncle, who is the youngest child of the little guys, is just six years older than me.

So, instead of having an uncle, I really grew up having an older brother who introduced me to many things. He was such a key fixture in my life as a young child.

Sports were and are one of the dynamics that brought the entire family together. I am sure sports is the glue that pulls and keeps a lot of families together. This is the beauty of sports and this is what it can and will do for people.

It brings people together. It helps people relate to one another and form lasting appreciation of one another. I believe athletics and the team atmosphere can break down racial barriers and cause a conversation of healing.

When I went to High School the school was predominantly white. Strange because I never gave it any thought in the choice of the school I was going to. The reason being was that as an athlete I had the opportunity that other freshmen didn't have to be social. When you are on a team the only thing that matters is knowing your responsibility and keeping the vision of the team. Meaning being a good teammate, doing my best so that my teammates would trust me and know that I had their back. Being on a team and going through drills tired, bruised and sore you find common ground with people that don't look like you.

Sports brought my uncle and I together early on, with my attending his games and his banquets. I was in the background and loved it all. To sit and watch someone that I was so close to be celebrated and decorated was amazing. Not only do I remember the games and all the impromptu family gatherings because of his athletic commitments, but I remember how it made me feel, coming to his games.

My Uncle was the star quarterback on a small-town high school team that nobody really expected anything from. But that team grew into the habit of taking down giants.

With a quality team like that, I'm sure the entire town was almost shutting down to come see them and be a part of the Friday night festivities. The energy that was produced from those Friday night games was dangerously contagious.

I was always intrigued by it and was an addict to it. It was a drug, and I would leave those games as a kid intoxicated with that energy.

What was that? How did they produce the kind of energy that so mesmerized me? I mean, it was everything. Since the quality of the team was so great, everything around it had to step up to a different level of excellence.

The band, the cheerleaders, the coaching all seemed to operate on a different level of excellence. The football field was set, it seems magically back in a corner next to the trees in the woods.
The announcer's voice seemed to echo throughout the entire town. I mean, Friday nights were an event and weekend activity by itself. That's all you saw on Friday nights, but so much more was conceived and birthed from that energy and that excitement that still lives today.

I ask questions about those times. Was it the level of attention that the athletes received that inspired me? Was it the people watching, cheering, and recognizing the players in town?

Maybe it was deeper than that. The whole team and the coaches were so disciplined, so committed, that the energy of being so focused on a goal became something that you could tangibly feel and catch if you were close enough to it.

I wanted to catch it, I wanted it all over me! I believe this is the responsibility of every person that is gifted and talented -- that you owe it to your gift to be so focused on being the best that the discipline that it takes is contagious. Without wanting to or trying to, my uncle's focus and discipline towards football conceived an energy and excitement that made me want to discover what was in me that could generate that same level of kinetic energy – the kind of energy that affected everybody that came close enough to me. Because my uncle played sports the way he did and at the level that he did, it injected me with a drive to compete. I was so close to him, but he was uncommon, because of what I would see from him and his teammates on a Friday night.

I would often sit there watching, or I would get up and play football on the side of the field with the other kids, who felt what I felt. There is no way we could sit still.

It was so amazing to be inspired by that level of energy. This is the same energy and excitement that generates millions of dollars. From commercials to a sneaker deal, this is the concept that keeps us creating.

COMMITMENT + DISCIPLINE CONCEIVES FOCUS that GENERATES EXCITEMENT that is CONTAGIOUS.

Be so committed and disciplined to your goal, that it will conceive a focus in you that generates a level of excitement that will affect the people around you.

Chapter 10

Relentle(s)s

pg.72

Swagger- to walk or strut with defiance

I can remember walking to the gym for basketball practice, just happy and excited to be on a team. I started playing at 10 years old at the Friars Club.

It was about a two to three mile walk from my house to the gym. Sometimes that walk was longer because I didn't start off well in the beginning. Sometimes I got a ride back home. Walking into that gym was a great feeling. I felt something walking into the Friars Club in the earlier 90s. Brown cobblestone covered the steps and the floor. The hallway walls leading up to the gym were covered with that same craftsmanship.

I was young and even more inexperienced than in my high school years. That walk seemed at times to be so lonely, so unsure and uncertain. Being that inexperienced and that unsure potentially can change how you walk into the gym and what your mental state is. There are a lot of things that can present themselves as a reason to be unsure when you're trying to pursue a goal.

It's possible to have ability and not have confidence in that ability. It's very possible to be extremely talented and have no mental assurance that you actually can do it.

The questions become:

Where does confidence come from?

Are you born with confidence?

Can somebody give you confidence?

Can things give you confidence?

Once you have confidence, can it be taken away?

As a child and teen, I struggled with insecurity and uncertainty. Why was that? I look back now to learn.

I was the tallest in my grade, probably the most athletic, so why did I ever second-guess myself and then feel insecure about anything? What was it that other people had, that I felt that I didn't?

Let's be clear. NO BODY CAN MAKE YOU INSECURE AND OR LOSE CONFIDENCE -- UNLESS YOU ALLOW IT.

Transparency is honesty that breaks you free.

Though I accomplished some things athletically, that lack of confidence and insecurity held me back in the past and I don't want it to hold anybody else back.

Most people prey on and take advantage of people who lack confidence and struggle with internal insecurity. If you are not confident, and if you let your own second guessing rule your thoughts, you will never reach your full potential.

I had too many questions and not enough action. The questions grew so many that it kept me from knowing how to act and or seeing the opportunity to act.

Insecurity - subject to fears, doubts; not self-confident or assured; not confident or certain; uneasy, anxious; not confident or certain; uneasy, anxious; not secure; exposed or liable to risk, loss, or danger; not firmly or reliably placed or fastened.

When you go into any new situation that you are not comfortable with, there is a period of questions and uncertainty. At this moment, you have to trust the process.

The beauty of time is that you can grow into some stuff and grow out of some stuff. During a period or season of uncertainty, don't let fears and things that are not very secure convince you that this is who you are. Even when it seems unstable and unsure, you have to be relentless enough to trust the process and keep going.

I always thought that arrogance is a waste of time. It can slow you down, almost like a weight vest. Even though you are moving, you are not able to move freely. Let's take a deeper look at the difference between confidence vs. arrogance.

What develops confidence in an individual?

For many, the difference between confidence and arrogance is complex, but I would suggest that the two go hand in hand. And most likely it would heavily depend on the individual that you're talking about; when you're talking about him or her; and in what situation. This doesn't provide a fair measuring tool to really define and understand the difference.

In general, arrogance flows from the heart, to promote and announce self. Confidence flows from the heart, standing on the stability of knowing who you are and what you were created to do.

Confidence conceives a character that has an appreciation for everything and everybody around. This becomes an explosive mindset.

Arrogance conceives a character that struggles to

exist and to have sustained happiness, when it's not all about them. You will not be able to consistently walk this way.

Arrogance forces you to stand on a foundation of things that will not hold you in position forever. Having real confidence places you on a foundation that you have grown into, understanding what matters most and which holds you in position forever.

In order to come out of a world of continuous questions and uncertainty, you will have to be still long enough to understand what is stable to stand on and what is not. Most don't appreciate the time to be still and discover what can be trusted to hold them steady.

I never understood how "successful people" could be so mean and nasty to people that are in pursuit of their own financial stability. I always wondered: If you are truly successful what are you mad about?

To walk in a more relentless way, you have to discover what is stable. It's crucial that you discover this. Being told what is stable is good and sets the groundwork for what is stable to exist. And stability is what gives strength to walk in this relentless way, through whatever situation and whatever environment you are in.

Here is the power that makes this walk so alive:

NOBODY HAS TO BELIEVE IT BUT YOU. IT IS NOT EVEN A REAL THING THAT OTHER PEOPLE HAVE TO BELIEVE, FOR IT TO EXIST AND HAPPEN IN YOUR LIFE.

TO BE CLEAR, HAVING A SUPPORT SYSTEM IS GREAT, HAVING PEOPLE THAT YOU CAN CONFIDE IN IS VERY HELPFUL. BUT YOU CANNOT DETERMINE THE FLOW OF YOUR WALK AND THE CONSISTENCY OF YOUR WALK BY HOW PEOPLE ARE AGREEING WITH IT. YOU HAVE TO ALLOW THE FRAMEWORK OF THE STABILITY TO CARRY YOU.

How do you identify what is stable? What beat do you set your walk to?

The discovery of what is stable is generated based on what your goals are and the priorities you set to reach those goals. This is your core and your core keeps you grounded and stable for any environment and any situation.

Even if the environment or situation may not start off in your favor; even if it looks like you will never recover stability in your priorities and the goals, you can still walk a certain way even before your goal comes alive.

Before anybody recognizes or awards you, your priorities and goals should already give indication of how amazingly relentless you are.

Chapter 11
Relentless(s)

pg.78

Steadfast - firmly fixed in place

To be steadfast is a conscious decision. There is a real
temptation in the world to quit and do something else, or worse to quit and do nothing. This state exists because things get harder and more of a challenge, as you progress toward your goal.

In the world we live in, there is a real temptation to give up. I have discovered that to complete the task and reach the goal, you have to resist this temptation when it is present.

But what does that mean and what does that look like on a daily basis? Being equipped to stand against the temptation to quit is key in this level of being relentless. If you want to be consistently relentless, you have to have this understanding.

The worst thing in the world is to look back on your life, your decisions and your behavior and have strong regret for most of the things that you have done. When you do that it can sentence you to a life of frustration.

You were not born to simply exist. You were not

born to experience hardship and simply accept that it is the end of your life.

Most people accept failure as final, and they offer no resistance to it. Who told you that was it? Who told you that your life was over because of one or a thousand mistakes?

There is something to learn and some way to grow from the worst of times. And it's OK for you to feel the temptation to quit and to feel like you are coming loose from your foundation. But it doesn't have to end just because you feel it.

Growing up in a competitive environment, I played in thousands of games -- which placed me in thousands of teachable moments. And you learn very quickly that you can never give up or quit until it is over.

No matter the circumstances of your life, you do not have to quit. Do not even entertain the temptation to quit and give up because it seems easier that way.

Everything seems difficult. And the truth is, it IS easier said than done, as the saying goes. But the reality is, that it can be done. Once you understand that reality, you can plan a strategy, and from the strategy you know how to act.

Another time that I quit in my life that I still relive and think about was when I was a sophomore in high school. For the first two years of high school

I played both football and basketball.
Although I already said that basketball was what I played in college, I also had the opportunity to play Division 1 Football.

Football was my father's sport of choice and he was a Division 1 college football quarterback at Miami University. (They were called the Redskins back then.), My maternal uncle was also a Division 1 college football player at Miami University. So, playing football was in my DNA.

By the time I got to 8th grade, I was on the radar and began playing AAU basketball for an elite traveling team out of Pittsburgh. So many amazing athletes came from that team.

I was placed on that team to be evaluated against the elite talent across the country. Evaluation really meant that the recruiting process for college basketball began for me that weekend I started playing with that team.

By the time I was a high school sophomore, I was on three different AAU teams, not including still being committed to my local school basketball summer schedule.

It was very tough and the level of sacrifice was high and very demanding. There was a lot that I missed, simply because I was out of town or coming back from being out of town playing basketball.

There was also the wear and tear on my body, only to gear up to play football in the fall. It was very difficult at 16 to do that and still stay focused.

So, I made an executive decision to not play football. That did not go over too well with the football coaching staff, my parents and parts of my family.

Essentially, I said I just didn't want to play football and wanted to focus on basketball. But really, I was saying I quit. It was the easy way out. Plus, I wanted my social life back.

As I look back at this situation, I realize that the reason why I continue to relive this moment in my life was that I really did want to play football.

And the thought of playing in high school and the potential of playing in college was intriguing. I had myself questions about that situation, and I wanted and needed answers.

The first question was: Why would a person ever give up on what he actually wanted to do?

This is what I learned. If you truly want to do something, you have to decide how bad you want it. If you do want it badly enough, you have to resist the temptation to quit and be patient until it works out.

As much as I wish I could go back and play football, I will never be able to go back to that space and time in my life. That time is gone and that decision is ingrained into my history.

But what remains is the opportunity to pull strength from that situation on how to be steadfast. This is something to learn, because life is tough and the troubles of life can reach the point where quitting seems the responsible thing to do.

But you cannot quit. You have to with all your might hold on to those goals you started with, hold tight to what your focus is and don't take your eyes off it. This is being relentless.

When you have it in your mind to quit and seek the easy way out every time it gets hard, that is not being **RELENTLESS**. It doesn't matter if it's your purpose, your career, your life as a parent, your marriage or the course of your life.

STAY FIXED IN ON IT!!!

Making the decision to only play basketball was the easy way out. That formed a pattern and an escape plan in me that manifested every time there was trouble.

But you can't quit, and you will not quit. You WILL remain focused. You will remain steadfast. And even in trouble and pressure, even being perplexed many times, continue to stand on your focus.

Resist the temptation to explain yourself to people who don't want to understand or appreciate your focus. You are wasting your precious energy.

Fight the temptation to isolate yourself from the world because you failed and/or quit before. No matter how many times you have called it quits and told yourself you would never be able to accomplish it, get back up and stand up.

When you stand up this time, focus on the goal with a grip that is securely tied to your purpose.

What you are focused on is key and makes or breaks your ability to stay firmly fixed in place. The lesson you learn in this is how to protect your focus.

You do not have to lose, and you are not going to quit. Stand in your focus. Hold tight to what you feel pushing you. Protect what you're looking at.

Implement change where it is needed. But for your future's sake, be steadfast and don't move from that position.

Take A Deep Breath and FOCUS

Conclusion

The vision of this project has been to empower you and to inspire you to reach as far as you can. I purposely have been transparent to show that you are not alone in facing internal obstacles.

As the author of this book, I designed it to challenge you. And after it has challenged you, I hope you have a clear strategy on how to move forward to attain your goals.

I also prayed for you – each and every reader of ***Take A Deep Breath and Focus***. I prayed that this book would truly inspire you to achieve great things. Inspiration is an interesting thing, because when real inspiration occurs, it causes life to happen.

You need to hear that you CAN be and do what you have dreamed of. It is my personal conviction that any person -- who is committed enough -- can overcome anything and achieve his goal. I personally believe ANYBODY can be what he or she wants to be.

Now the question is: Exactly how do you remove, go around or go under the obstacles you face to achieve your purpose and destiny?

Vision is the key. It's very difficult to achieve or move forward, if you don't have a vision of where you are going. Most people can't see where they want to go until it's right in front of them.

The majority of people won't reach their destination. That's because they think they have to have all the resources they need right away, or they think everybody they care about must believe they can really do it.

There is a small group of people – a minority group of humanity -- that I would love for you to become a part of. They don't have the resources and they don't have the favor of all the "right" people, but they achieve their goals anyway. I've seen it happen. And it can happen for you – if you believe it will.

As you know, when I was in high school I started playing varsity basketball as a freshman. My body was ready for that, but my mind wasn't. Well, during sophomore year it was evident that my mind had started to catch up.

All I wanted to do was dunk and keep dunking. I put a strategy together and all I did was think about dunking. I thought about it so much at night that my heart rate would go up. I would see it in my mind, and it was so real thinking about it.

It seems crazy, but after dunking over and over again so many times in my mind, when I got into the game, I would just make it happen. It was so satisfying to see it actually happen.

So, here's how to achieve it -- whatever it is you want. First, it has to exist in your thoughts, and you have to see it alive and happening in your mind.

Mind over matter suggests that nothing is too big to challenge the focus of the position your mind takes. No matter what voices, no matter what the obstacles are, they are no match for you when you put your mind to it. If you can get it in your mind that it's already achieved, you'll eventually have it in reality. There is a habit that you are forming, and it is consistency.

Remember...

You must evaluate the situation -- as quickly as you can -- to identify the issue that is stopping you from reaching your goal. There is no time for excuses and/or blaming anybody for the obstacle that you face.

There is a power that you have and that is to make an adjustment based on what you have identified as the problem. When you have honestly identified the issue, you will have a clear understanding of how to make those necessary adjustments.

There is a formula that produces unstoppable focus: COMMITMENT plus DISCIPLINE. This combination conceives a level of focus that generates a level of excitement that is contagious.

You have a responsibility to focus on, so that those who are depending on you for leadership and direction you will be inspired and strengthened.

My big feet do not fit in your small shoes.

It is okay for your purpose to not agree with other people's vision of what success is and what success looks like. You will frustrate yourself by trying to keep up with everybody's ideal of success. Who is to say that what is for me is for you and what is for you is for me. Who is to say that the route you took is the route that we all should take to fulfill purpose. There is fatal danger in a copy and paste life without any edit and or personal reflection. Fatal because a copy and paste never includes context and the why. Give us context with your life by being authentically you. It's not fair to the people you were created to inspire, when you only do what other people are comfortable with you doing.

The challenge is that you have to go, live, dream and reach while being misunderstood and underappreciated. Think about it, how can we even put the pressure on people to understand and support something that is not proven and or fully developed. It's subconsciously saying agree with me and sign off on it so that I can believe in it. That's not the way it's going to work. It may hurt your feelings but it will not stop you from being who you were created to be.

There are so many things that can define us and become a personal logo that projects to the world who we are. If we are not careful we will allow insignificant things to define who we are and if we are relevant to the world or not. I would even caution you even in your pursuit to fulfill why you were created, to not use a depreciated criteria that will not produce the essentials of life. There may be an argument on what are the essentials of life. Some may not find use of these essentials while others may hold them sacred. Interesting how criteria become so crucial depending on who is giving the criteria.

I never had a complex about the size of my feet but the truth is I didn't understand the significance of my size. When you are surrounded in an environment that is opposite of what you look like, it's hard to find confidence. Where do you find confidence to be you when everything is different. The mistake I made was that I thought my feet had to be the majority size (that is around you) in order to be perfect. My feet were big and there was nothing that I could do about it. What I didn't understand is that later it would be a benefit and my big feet were essential to being tall.

I confess that I fell victim to this dynamic and I tried to put my big feet into smaller shoes. I suffered alot and every time I thought I could take it, I would have to take the shoes and let my toes stretch back out. Funny now but extremely painful then. Every time you decide to put your big feet literally and or figuratively in smaller shoes you will suffer. What is worse than the pain is eventually your feet shrink and conform to the smaller size. You will never be able to regain the size of your big feet and or big ideals that you had. Here is the lesson that your big feet will never fit their small shoes. Do not give up on your dreams because it seems not to fit what is popular.

More forward with relentless behavior:
Realizing + Implementing +Repetition

I dedicated this book to Kingston Levi McIntosh, dream big and believe in God even bigger.

I dedicated this book to my mother and father, who both made many sacrifices. You both together gave me the balance that I needed to be RELENTLESS!

To my sister, niece, my nephew and my entire on both sides KEEP DREAMING!

To my entire family both immediate and extended I pray that through the pages of this book you dream and are inspired to go and BE RELENTLESS.

When was the last time you dreamed so big that it made you nervous? I charge you to keep dreaming and reaching far beyond where you are.

I have a question for you. What caused you to stop dreaming?

I want you to make a list for your eyes only, 3 things that have caused you to stop pursuing your dreams.

1.

2.

3.

Now that you have made a list of reasons and or distractions that have come up against your dreams. I want you to in the space provided below to dream a little.

Short term goals...
(Within the next year)

Long term goals...
(within 5-10)

My encouragement to you is to understand words have power. The words that come out of your mouth live in your future. So the caution here is choosing your words wisely. I want you to choose wisely for your future's sake.

I challenge you to be relentless enough to start speaking all your dreams into reality. This is your divine birthright as a created being to DREAM BIG!!!

BE RELENTLESS

Made in the USA
Columbia, SC
13 September 2023

22820921R00057